# BLUE

# LIKE

# THE

# HEAVENS

# Books by Gary Gildner

## Poetry

*Blue Like the Heavens: New & Selected Poems*     1984
*The Runner*     1978
*Nails*     1975
*Digging for Indians*     1971
*First Practice*     1969

## Limited Editions

*Jabón*     1981
*Letters from Vicksburg*     1976
*Eight Poems*     1973

## Anthology

*Out of This World: Poems from the Hawkeye State*     1975

## Fiction

*The Crush*     1983

# BLUE LIKE THE HEAVENS

New & Selected Poems

## GARY GILDNER

University of Pittsburgh Press

Published by the University of Pittsburgh Press, Pittsburgh, Pa. 15260
Copyright © 1984, Gary Gildner
All rights reserved
Feffer and Simons, Inc., London
Manufactured in the United States of America


**Library of Congress Cataloging in Publication Data**

Gildner, Gary.
  Blue like the heavens.

  I. Title.
PS3557.I343B55   1984       811'.54       83-19746
ISBN 0-8229-3490-6
ISBN 0-8229-5358-7 (pbk.)

The author and publisher wish to express their grateful acknowledgments to the following publications, in which some of these poems originally appeared: *The Above Ground Review*, *Aisling*, *The American Review*, *Counter/Measures Magazine*, *December*, *Epoch*, *Foxfire*, *The Georgia Review*, *Kansas Quarterly*, *The New Salt Creek Reader*, *Occident*, *The Paris Review*, *Shenandoah*, *Sumac*, and *Transpacific*.

"It's Spring, Lover" originally appeared in *Abraxas/Chowder Special Issue*, 14/15. "Letters from Vicksburg" was first published in *Antaeus*. "Letter to a Substitute Teacher" is reprinted from *The Antioch Review*. "The Man and the Goshawk" first appeared in *Crazy Horse*. "Around the Horn," "Heart Attack," "Nails," and "Passion Play" are reprinted from *Field*. "Around the Kitchen Table" and "Prayer for My Father" were originally published in *Great Lakes Review*. "For Judy" and "The Last Monarch of the Season" are reprinted from *The Laurel Review*. *Lillabulero* was first publisher of "The House on Buder Street" and "The Girl in the Red Convertible." "The Shy Roofer" is reprinted from *The Nation*. "Blue Like the Heavens," "Ice Shanties," "In the Beginning," "In the Social Security Office," "Johann Gaertner (1793–1887)," "A Memory," "My Father After Work," and "Today They Are Roasting Rocky Norse" originally appeared in *New Letters*. "Eeny, Meeny, Miney, Mo, Miss Beech" is reprinted from *The North American Review*. "Edward" and "A Letter from My Good Hand" were first published in *Northwest Review*. "Jabón" first appeared in *Poetry*. *Poetry Now* originally published "The High-Class Bananas," "Old Farm in Northern Michigan," and "Statistics."

The following poems first appeared in *Poetry Northwest*: "After World War II," "Burn-Out," "The Day Before Thanksgiving, A Call Comes to Me Concerning Insulation," "A Field Mouse at My Fishing Hole," "Harold Fogel Could Be Anywhere," "Last Articles," "Life & Death in Skokie," "Mark Only One Circle," "Poem with Levels of Meaning," "Poems," "The Porch," "That Summer," "They Have Turned the Church Where I Ate God," "Toads in the Greenhouse," and "Xmas."

*The publication of this book is supported by grants from the National Endowment for the Arts in Washington, D.C., a Federal agency, and the Pennsylvania Council on the Arts.*

*for* Judy and Gretchen

# CONTENTS

# CONTENTS

# CONTENTS

Gary
Gildner

# First
# practice

1969

# FIRST PRACTICE

After the doctor checked to see
we weren't ruptured,
the man with the short cigar took us
under the grade school,
where we went in case of attack
or storm, and said
he was Clifford Hill, he was
a man who believed dogs
ate dogs, he had once killed
for his country, and if
there were any girls present
for them to leave now.
                              No one
left. OK, he said, he said I take
that to mean you are hungry
men who hate to lose as much
as I do. OK. Then
he made two lines of us
facing each other,
and across the way, he said,
is the man you hate most
in the world,
and if we are to win
that title I want to see how.
But I don't want to see
any marks when you're dressed,
he said. He said, *Now.*

# WEAN POEM

The day my parents tried to wean me
not because it was the Depression certainly
but because I was going on three
their apartment house caught fire
and burned to the ground. I didn't
have anything to do with it naturally
( a man on relief was smoking in bed )

but my mother saved me and her ratty
muskrat coat by putting two and two together
and the next day at a relative's
my father, who is noted for his composure under stress,
broke out a bottle of Four Roses he couldn't afford
and more excited, I am told, than the day I was born
invited everybody in to have a drink with me.

# EDWARD

I knew him by a huge stomach laugh,
strange tumors on his arms,
and a Chippewa arrowhead he said he won
from the crafty Ojibway — in a turkey shoot
attended by many braves in bearskin.
I shuddered. My mother called him "Dutchman,"
baked him beans with sweet cuts of ham fat;
I learned he liked to watch her nurse me,—
his own sons had grown old too fast,
his daughters were too nervous.

Now I sniff his sons' cigar smoke, recall
he sent me with a dime to buy "one for you
and one for me"— there was an owl on the box.
I mixed the nails in his bins, learned
to swear "God damn to pot!"— and more,
which made my mother shudder.
Then we left to take another job.
His lumber yard could only hold two sons.

I look around his wood room, see
a single high-top boot, a tattered
*True Detective*. Will they use it,
whoever takes the place, to someday start a fire?
There are no relics of our trips to Gaylord.
I cannot smell the pine, nor find
on the magazine victim's yellow breasts
the blue, lusty eye that caught my first goshawk.
I hear the wind against the hill
his fat, protected deer fed at,
and perhaps the echo of a real wail
too far off— but nothing else below
the noisy time upstairs that matters.

# LETTER TO A SUBSTITUTE TEACHER

Dear Miss Miller,
You are someone
too sweet to sleep alone
and I can't help myself

sitting here hearing
your soft voice so
I must tell you
I like you

very much and would like
to know you better.
I know there is a difference
in our age and race

but we do have something
in common—You're a girl
and I'm a boy
and that is all

we need. Please
do not look at me
like I'm silly or sick
and most of all

please do not reject
my very first love
affair. If you do
not feel the same

as I do please
tell me how I can forget
your unforgettable voice
that reminds me

of Larry the Duke's pet
birds in the morning,
your blue eyes like the
Blessed Virgin's,

your golden hair and your
nice red mouth. Please
give me some sign
of how you feel,

I would rather be hurt
than forgotten forever.
Sincerely yours,
The Boy in the Green Shirt.

# SZOSTAK

I list you from the past with food
I carry home in sacks, to keep me
going—nothing more. I lie of course

but that's the truth. You died
at one A.M.—reading Conrad
in the can by kerosene.

I write this straight, my friend,
as straight as you walked
home from Standish with your nightly pint

of whiskey. Well, we waited
for the priest; wool trousers
made me itch; the hair

was trimmed above your lip. I recalled
that cake crumbs at a wedding
stuck in it—and how, when slicing up

a pig, you spit tobacco juice. Beyond
your head a satin pillow read
(in pink) "TO MY LOVING MOTHER";

under this a heart
(deep red) along which crawled a fly. Some fool
put pennies on your eyes. Assisted by the priest,

your wife knelt down, began her beads.
Her pretty nieces from Chicago followed, giving off
a cherry smell

that cured the kerosene. Old Pole,
I couldn't cry. That wasn't you. You'd been kicked
by mares, wore scars,

forked out shit. Secretly I scratched
my balls, then took the first slim silky pair
of legs I saw, and cooled us in your creek.

# THE SHY ROOFER

This roofer works at night
on the sly—
he's only a shy man.
Nails, tar, squares covered
and uncovered: these
he proffers quickly,
automatically,
by hand.
It's the moon that's
on his mind, gentlemen—
the stars, the
ladies turning over
one more time
to show their lips,
their honest
hips,
to whisper
in their sleep
you're doing fine,
roofer.

# POEMS

I sent my mother copies of my poems in print
to show her I was not a complete failure
and could do something besides
write dirty stories, and she was so happy

she replied with a poem of her own
about her heart waiting for spring and the beautiful
blue sky and some other lovelies
I don't remember, without calling it a poem

but you could tell that's what it was
because she lined it all out. The prettiest part
of her letter, however, was the end
where she said in her own true voice

"but mainly I can't wait for spring
because then my old man can get
to his garden and won't be bellyaching—
Oh he'll track in dirt and his hands

will never be clean and his breath
you can bet will be one big onion
once they get ripe, but it makes you
feel so good in your bones and it's all free!"

# MY COED WIFE

My coed wife
reading Lenin
leggy

in her tight red
bathing suit
under

cool water-
colored
pears

is enough
science
for one

afternoon.

# TO MY DAUGHTER

Not counting the little kids
you shock everyone you know
calling me Gary and Judy Judy
no one thinks it's natural
let alone healthy so we
better keep the pleasure
we get from filling
your balloons with water
and squirting the dogs when they
come to lick us in the tub
quiet, lover.

# FOR JUDY

I was trying to write the perfect poem
having been rejected on the only decent
day that month—it didn't stink
and it didn't rain behind my eyes—

when, hanging out the clothes,
you turned and faced this failure—
waving the wind from your hair,
being the best of reasons.

Poems by Gary Gildner

1971

# GEISHA

The boxer bitch is pregnant
puffed up like an Oriental wrestler!

The boys stand back,
aloof, embarrassed
or unsure of their hands.

But the girls, their cheeks aflame,
are down on shiny knees
praising all the nipples.

# HAROLD FOGEL COULD BE ANYWHERE

The girls of St. Mary's school
were given in puberty
three all-embracing (legal,
religious) rules.

One, do not wear
patent leather shoes.
They reflect
your underwear.

Remember the man
who looked at his face
in the pool too long?
Dead as a cat.

Next, never forget to take
a newspaper
when later
you go on a date.

In case
he should ask you
to sit on his lap—
there is his napkin!

Question? Oh,
you understand;
thank you.
Three, after filling

the tub
sprinkle the surface
with talcum.
This will, believe us,

eliminate visions
when getting in.
Now, one more thing
before you go: God

in all His glory
made the trees—
and they are good
and even necessary.

But from vast
experience we know
that little boys can
shinny up in nothing flat

—especially
when little girls
are walking down below.
So remember, please

keep fast
around the neck,
not to mention
everywhere.

# EENY, MEENY, MINEY, MO, MISS BEECH

I loved Miss Beech
my kindergarten teacher
hard enough to give up spitting
in the fishbowl,
hard enough to lick
her yellow hair in dreams
for years. She told us doves
were gentle, wolves
were mean. I believed
everything she whispered.
Then one day I saw
the raw body of a dove
its mate, in heat, had flayed alive.
I hunted down a book
and read that fighting wolves
have something in their blood
to cool it,
even when the weaker gives
its vein.
Oh Miss Beech, that night
I offered you my bone.
You took it in your hands
and broke it.

# THE FARM

I watch the old barn lean
and think: *the swallows will hold it up*
*and in an emergency run*
*screaming for help*
then turn toward the creek
the Prince Albert can on my hip.
I'd found it, faded to a light rosé,
in a heap of harnesses and junk.
Once, we'd fill these bright
red cans with crawlers
and a chunk of dirt for perch
and bass and pike.
Never suckers: those we took
the hayforks after, working
squeeze plays on them
at the wide, pebbly turn
where the creek goes shallow—
and freeze our feet and shins
by staying in too long
but hardly wince, flipping
sucker after sucker up the bank
and fiercely keeping score.
Later, kneeling in the sun
we'd slice their bellies
and like crazy doctors slip
the long creamy tapeworms out.
We tossed the worms at trees
or hung them over posts
to treat the crows,

as up the hill we hauled our catch
going past the wet-nosed bull
whose cock our cousin showed us
was a slim pink sword
by offering the bull a milker's
bony haunch (our city eyes bugged out
but she just chewed her cud and drooled)—
and at the pigpen
handed in our kill, quick
to keep our fingers from the old sow's snout.
Then we hit the fields for fat
tomatoes, cucumbers and radishes
—and down the hill again
to wash them in the creek, chasing
with our cuke torpedoes
schools of minnows—
and remember suddenly
to check between our toes
for oily bloodsuckers;
always finding some, we'd scrape
them off with sand (and pray
that none had crawled
in our ears
or up our butts when swimming.)

On the bridge we sprawled
across the logs and ate, reciting
batting averages; the truly great
were always dead—except for
maybe Williams and DiMaggio . . .
and getting up we'd sprint
toward the woods, where uncles
flashing lights last fall
froze deer before the season,
and over whiskey and smoked sturgeon bragged
how sweet the corn-fed bucks
whose pricks were never used,—
then stopping, taking off our shirts, a leaf
of wintergreen between our teeth,
we'd lie on moss
or soft pine needles, lazily
bring down a hawk
with sticks of birch that served as 30–30's,
or just peel them,
and slowly start to dream
of sending daring messages,
written on the stiff clean bark.

# THE GIRL IN THE RED CONVERTIBLE

The girl in the red convertible
with the heater going full blast
and her throat knocking
turns off the lights
on the road to Winterset
and rolls toward the moon
resting expressionless
on the next hill.

When the car stops coasting
it is still June, and
she is at the edge
of a field, waiting . . .
She has a
"fifty-fifty chance." It—
that expression—is quietly
eating her eyeballs . . .

At dawn a cow appears; then
another. Taking all the time
they need. If only something
would break—break open
so she could scream—
Finally there are nine lined up
along the fence—
like visitors to the zoo.

# MARK ONLY ONE CIRCLE

Mark only one circle.
Mark "hot water" even if you have it only part time.
Are you white, black, Japanese, or Other?
If you are "Other" print race.
If you are Indian print tribe.
Erase mistakes completely.

Have you ever been knocked out?
How long were you unconscious?
Did it hurt?
Did it hurt very much, not very much, none of these?
Does anyone outside the immediate family use your "facilities"?

If you went down for the count, did your mouth volunteer
    tiny bubbles?
Did anyone giggle?
Did a lady in a sporelike lavender hat
    or an ape in red suspenders kick
    a midget popcorn vendor full
    speed on the knee
    because they couldn't see around him?

Have you ever wanted to drown your sorrows?
Are you sick and tired of being out of shape?
Are you sick and tired of dropping your guard?
If elected, will you promise not to come back?

# RUSTLING A HOG

### 1

Arrive
at night.
Bring beer in case
you have to wait
— some son of a bitch might
be outside leaking, screwing
off or something.

Speak
in pig-talk.
Don't leave clues, like wing
your cans around.
Also, winter's bad —
snow & polka dots.
Pull it off in fall.

Choose a juicy
young one. Ordinarily a ball-
peen hammer *wap!*
between the eyes
(that soft spot there)
will do the job.
Then blow.

**2**

Clean & bleed it.
Dig a pit & fire charcoal.
Man, don't forget

the bastard's wormy—
turn him
till he's crisp.

By the fire
drop, from time to time, a gob of spit
& tell your story.

Watch your girl
feel her jeans & wiggle.
Cut the sweetmeat loose,

trim it.
Notice how your spaniel flops
& laps her crotch.

She's nervous. After eating
suck your fingers,
check around. Pick your teeth.

# MY MOTHER WRITES . . .

My mother writes to wonder
why I missed Christmas
on top of Thanksgiving—
she brought a turkey up

from the freezer
baked a juicy ham
and, if I can imagine, peeled
sweet potatoes, onions, luscious Idahoes

and beets beets beets until
my father asked, "Are you crazy?"
No, but someday

the blood will squirt
from her head and face
because the pills she takes for the zooming pressure
are breaking her heart

and nothing tastes like it used to
if I can imagine.

# HEART ATTACK

The day
my father's heart attacked
and knocked him down
in Michigan,

I was pulling huskies
off a woodchuck
in a thicket up in Canada—
he'd turned to make a stand,

having lost his balance.
There was nothing left
except the claws,
a rag of fur,

and blood,
like makeup,
on the lead dog's smiling
stuffed-toy face.

Later,
when I got the call
from home,
they told me not to worry—

he was plugged in
to the best machine, and a nurse's eyes
were on him
day and night.

I downed
two shots of bourbon, felt
my chest contract,
and then

at fifteen thousand feet
I watched a blonde
with fuzz above her lip
pass out pin-on wings

to balding lovers
buckled in the belly.
Then I slept,
dreaming that we touched

down in Flint,
where I found him
wired
to a television set.

The doctor said,
"We call this level line his heart."
I was afraid
to shake his hand,

the hand
that showed me how to hold
a hammer,
and sat down;

his nails,
shiny as a baby's,
lay between us.
Overhead, the chalkline hummed

in blue.
Fifteen minutes passed.
I tried to kiss him
but I couldn't move my lips.

"Remember the day
I kicked snow in your face?
How you squealed!
And I kept thinking you meant

*go faster—faster—*"
The nurse reared up
—"Go easy"—
then sat back

and rolled her eyes,
as if she'd heard that story too!
He lowered his voice—a good boy—
and whispered

he couldn't stand
or breathe without feeling
the ice
coming up in his lungs—

and falling,
falling into head-high drifts
he wished
for something warm to wear—

and grabbed
my hunting shirt.
I woke,
we were on the ground.

A girl's hand
was pinned against my chest,
and she was crying, "Please,
oh please let go—"

# DIGGING FOR INDIANS

The first week the soil was clean,
except for a shrew's lobster-
colored jaw, a bull snake caught
in its long final bellow,
and an ocher mouse holding
its head, as if our trowels had given it
a migraine. Then we hit bird-bone
beads, clam shells,

and then we struck a spine.
Digging slowly we followed it
north, toward a stand of cottonwood
overlooking the river and, beyond,
a patch of abandoned pickups and plows
taking the sun.
We stopped
below the shoulder blades for lunch.

Then we resumed, working down
and into the body,
now paring
the dirt like exotic fruit,
now picking between the ribs
as if they were bad teeth
aching with impacted meat.
We were dripping wet,

and slapping at sweat bees
attacking the salt
on our backs—
but he was taking shape,
he was beginning to look,
as his pelvis came through,
like a man. We uncovered
his thighs and brittle, tapering feet,

and then we went for his skull.
Shaving close, slicing off
worms that curlicued
like brains out of place,
we unearthed his hollow expression,
his bony brow,
and finally, in back of his neck,
an arrowhead stuck to the vertebrae.

The ground rumbled under our knees—
Quickly we got the Polaroid
and snapped him from several angles—
except for the scattered fingers
we could not have planned a better specimen . . .
Then we wrapped him up in foil.
Tomorrow we would make a plaster cast,
and hang it in the junior college.

# MEETING THE REINCARNATION ANALYST

I guess because it was Key West
and I was a little drunk
I expected some ridiculous facsimile
of Sidney Greenstreet, puffing hard, to slip
through the beaded curtains first—
to set me up with secrets smirking
on his sweaty mug.

But nobody like that came in
to the Immortality Consultation Room
off Whitehead Street that smelled
of incense, salt, and cat shit—
just Patricia Peel, Ph.D.,
the mystic in a flaming beehive
hairdo, teardrop earrings, and a sheet.

She offered me her hand—snakes and snappers,
swordfish, flies and eyeballs
—these were on the rings
her fingers wiggled at me.
On the middle knuckle of her middle
finger, dominating all the fauna,
was a baby's skull, in gold.
I kissed her blue-veined wrist.

She said, "Please sit"—
and pointed to the satin sofa.
At my side she opened up her sheet
to show a copper cross inlaid
with writhing octopuses
hanging down between her breasts.
"You have," she said, "six former lives
and many, many Karmic ties—"

I interrupted: "Have you really got a Ph.D.?"
She continued, "—and in each past life

you loved an evil woman."
The first, reported Dr. Peel, was a Carib maiden
taken by Cortez to entertain him
on the voyage back to Spain . . .
"She succumbed to lust, disease, and worms."

My mystic gripped her cross.
"The second girl, a Salem witch,
accused of lying down with pigs—"
"Hey wait a minute," I said.
But Dr. Peel spoke on, her eyes
as hard and green as early walnuts,
killing off my Salem witch by stuffing
down her throat her lovers' testicles.

An octoroon of Jefferson's
who later slept with Madison,
and a Cajun who was burned
alive with John Wilkes Booth
were my ladies three and four
and I had had it. I dropped
the Consultation fee in Patty's lap, and left.

That night, in my air-conditioned Holiday,
I showered with a smiling bonefish—
then fixed a gin and tonic,
and watched debilitated Ponce de León
arrive in Florida at Eastertide
above my bed. Oh, I'd love to say
she came around without her junk,
and that we had a laugh, and maybe
even said what we were looking for.
But the truth is no one came,
and the next day I moved on.

# 8/22/38—8/22/68

What did you do last summer?
Last summer I turned the corner.

What did you think about?
Tad Weed—who weighed 116 pounds and booted
goals for Ohio State.

Did you ever try anything foolish?
Once I tried a drop-kick and missed.

Were you a hit in high school?
The coach flinched and called me a fool.

What did you do on your birthday?
Kept in touch.

What else?
Sold my Austin-Healey, felt sorry.

What else?
Practiced my craft, ground my teeth.

What else?
Missed my calling.

What else?
Ate hard-boiled eggs with angry horseradish,
feisty leeks and cold sliced tomatoes.

How did you feel?
Ready.

What for?
Albacore tuna and tender green peas
in a butter and onion and pepper white sauce.

Then what?
The sun settled down behind Audubon, Iowa.

How did you feel?
No bigger than a minute.

# THE LAST MONARCH OF THE SEASON

When I come back
with it in my hands

careful not to bruise the color
of its life

release it to the pillow, say
that I have touched

its trembling only—

When I come back
and lay my lips

uncovered
near its wings

and put your fingers
over them forever

once again—

When I do all of this
in prelude to your kiss

will you let me go
in the morning?

# NA⊥LS

GARY GILDNER

1975

# THE HOUSE ON BUDER STREET

My father found it after the war—
five rooms and two long rows of purple grapes
beside the picket fence in back
—which Eddie Hill, holding his jewels, leaped
the night we peppered a township
cruiser with bird-shot cut
from shotgun shells and stuffed in our BB rifles.

Every summer my mother made grape jelly
and Eddie, who had it down pat, polished my curve ball.
Up in his attic we gagged on rum-soaked Crooks;
he described taking a flashlight to bed
and crawling under the sheets
the nights he slept with his older half-sister.
Our houses were back to back.

The Buder Street brain was Jerry Skellinger.
He had a wing like a chicken
but could figure a Tiger's average without a stick or paper.
Once throwing darts I got him in the shoulder.
His father taught math and after school put peacocks
and roses in blocks of clear plastic.
They had a black cocker named Silly.

The night my brother was born
my father and I slept in the basement—
on Grandma's brass bed hauled down from the farm.
I was afraid of spiders
and clung to his back.
My aunt Sophie came from Detroit and steamed bottles
and made my sister and me eat everything.

I thought I'd be a doctor.
I took a kitchen knife and cut the cry
thing from my sister's doll. She screamed.
My aunt sighed Be constructive.
I filled a can with polliwogs from Miller's Pond.
I watched Shirley Fox bite her warts.
Shirley came from Arkansas; her parents hated Catholics.

When my brother could toddle he climbed
a ladder and fell on his liver.
Then he picked up hepatitis.
When he got on his feet we lit sparklers
and buried hot stones to bake potatoes.
Shirley's warts were gone, too.
She'd lifted a robin's egg and rubbed on bloody bird.

Now we needed a bigger house.
Bigger also meant better.
My mother hated the dusty unpaved street,
the soot from the coal-burning furnace;
and her fruit cellar was packed!—
she couldn't can another pickle.
Some nights my father slept in our room.

The fall my mother insisted I still needed
long underwear, I threw them at her.
My father knocked me down,
then grabbed a long-handled hammer
and began to hit the house.
The rest of us cleaned up the chips.
By winter we had a new bedroom.

In the spring Shirley's breasts appeared.
Eddie worked on my slider and Miller's Pond
was filled in to build what my father called cracker boxes;
they were painted orange and lime and raspberry sherbet.
Some of Shirley's kin from Arkansas moved in one.
They went to work for Fisher Body, like her father,
and called each other shop rats.

My sister and I attended the Catholic school—
everyone else went to public. Eddie reported
that Shirley crossed her legs in Algebra; he figured
to make All-County and carried Trojans in his wallet.
My mother counted the Baptists on the street.
My father called it harping.
Sunday drives meant looking for a lot.

# AFTER WORLD WAR II

We piled in the car
& went for a ride!
My mother wore lipstick,
my father wore slippers
& the kids poked their heads
out the window & giggled
at people kissing.
Later we stopped
at a Bo-Kay stand & punched
each other in the fuzzy back seat
while waiting for seven flavors.
Then my father lit up, my mother
blotted her lips,
and we pulled into
Country Club Lane
which went in a circle under the moon,
and we promised to behave —
and look at the dark
brick houses, the long
carpet lawns feeding little brown deer,
and the *swoosh*        *swoosh*
of sprinklers
and the colored cars, and a lady
wearing high yellow hair and holding
a little white cup,
out strolling a yellow dog
that looked back at us
until we were out of sight.

# AROUND THE KITCHEN TABLE

Around the kitchen table we are never out
of shape, grinning back the skinned and bleeding
shins we picked up in our first front yards,
remembering the black and blue, the sweaty
run-ins with the nuns who always had our number,
recalling how we counted time by cornsilk
curling from our burning corners,
by the hams and sausage Grandpa strung
around the smokehouse, by the smelt
we shoveled in the car and drove all night with,
breathing stars and silos, breathing whispers
in the scarves the girls gave us, counting time
by frost and field mice, by weddings and the necks
of roosters Grandma wrung to welcome us back home
—and all the while we're talking loaves of Polish
rye going down with butter, beer, and links
of steaming kielbasa! And everyone weeps
unable to keep his hands off the horseradish.
Then Uncle John, whose knees are pocked
with shrapnel, makes up his mind on the spot
to polka with Uncle Andy, the stiff one
who wears gartered socks. And gathered around
like this, someone always recalls a relation
burdened with more than his share of grief,
and the latest passing, the latest operation.
But always there is food on the table
and always another wedding in sight—
a beautiful cousin with red hair—
and Uncle Joe will pick up Grandma and
look! already Grandma has her glass of beer,
blushing as the young blond Polish priest
bites into his chicken right beside her.

# NAILS

My father, his mouth full of nails,
is building my mother's dream house.

My mother is listing the grief
it cost her, & pointing out how smooth

the woodwork is. To her brothers:
well, the blacks are taking over —

& her cousins passing through from Santa Monica
swear the church is kissing ass. Ah,

a dream house draws the line on many
fronts. (St. Monica, if I remember, wed thou thee

a pagan, no? & brought him in the fold.
& when he died thou set

to work on sonny boy, old dissolute Augustine, right?
Any food in there for thought?)

Meanwhile, time to pour
the basement floor,

& the Ready Mix man plops
his concrete through the future

rec room window, *Lord*
it isn't wet enough to spread!

Just lays there like a load some giant chicken
dropped. My father, mixing figures,

says all hell will hit the fan
if our fannies do not *move*

& sets my little brother on it with the hose
while we grab hoes & shovels, Lord

I liked that part & afterwards
the lump all smooth

we drank our beer & pop
& mopped our sweat,

& talked about What Next.
The future meant:

cut the lumber square,
make the nails go straight

& things will hold.
I loved that logic, saw him prove it —

then he said we're done
& covered up the last nail's head

with wood paste;
everything was smooth.

I moved around a lot
when I left home, making stories up.

In one blockbuster there's a lady says:
"You taste like roofing nails, father."

And: "You're growing shorter!"
Terrific dialogue but not much plot.

Like building dream houses —
no one knows what you mean.

# THEY HAVE TURNED THE CHURCH WHERE I ATE GOD

They have turned the church where I ate God
and tried to love Him into a gym

where as an altar boy I poured water and wine
into the pastor's cup, smelling the snuff
under his lip on an empty stomach

where I kept the wafer away from my teeth
thinking I could die straight to the stars
or wherever it was He floated warm and far

where I swung the censer at Benedictions to the Virgin
praying to better my jump shot from the corner
praying to avoid the dark occasions of sin

where on Fridays in cassock and Windsor knot and flannel pants
I followed Christ to His dogwood cross
breathing a girl's skin as I passed, and another's
trying less and less to dismiss them

where I confessed my petty thefts and unclean dreams
promising never again, already knowing
I would be back flushed with desire and shame

where I stood before couples scrubbed and stiff
speaking their vows, some so hard at prayer
I doubted they could go naked, some so shiny
I knew they already did it and grinned like a fool

where I stood before caskets flanked by thick candles
handing the priest the holy water
feeling the rain trickle down to my face
hearing the worms gnaw in the satin and grinding my teeth

where once a mother ran swooning to a small white box
and refused to let go calling God a liar screaming
to blow breath back in her baby's lungs

They have turned the church where I ate God
into a gym with a stage

where sophomores cross themselves before stepping
on soapboxes for the American Legion
citizenship prize
just as I crossed myself before every crucial free throw
every dream to be good

where on Friday afternoons in the wings
janitors gather to shuffle the deck
or tell what they found in a boy's locker wrapped in foil
or in a girl's love letter composed like maidenhair

where I can imagine pimpled Hamlets
trying to catch chunky Gertrudes at lies
no one believes in except the beaming parents

They have turned the church where I ate God
and tried to love Him into a gym with a stage
where now in my thirty-fourth year I stop
and bend my knee
to that suffering and joy I lost, that play
of pure confusion at His feet.

# PRAYER FOR MY FATHER

That gleaming boat they took the time and grief
to christen with carnations and the shakes
of holy water,
let it go.
And let the pain go with it.
Let it stay down there below the roots intact,
a tribute to the undertaker.
Let him join it.
And let my father stand
as in this photograph—
planted to his hips in current, holding up a bucketful of smelt
and beaming, as if any second he might fly!

Let him fly—
and let that blur, a child's hand that fluttered into view
when he looked up,
fly with him.

# PASSION PLAY

I am the son who steers his father's chair, his hawk
    fingers caressing a nugget of nitroglycerin

We are ten angels in two straight lines, under the eyes
    of a woman who wears a fox

We are a pair of clerics
    who wager the Pirates have all the guns

I am the one with a good nose
    I smell camel manure, sawdust, urine, sperm

I am a girl with marvelous legs, because of me
    men groan in their sleep, palm their throbbing hearts

I am a boy in spotless white bucks
    she has promised me her blood

I am a child with chalk for bones, I am tied flat
    they oil my crank, they point me in the right direction

We are the ones who twitch and shiver and drip
    our nerves are a joke

I am blind, I squeeze
    a rubber ball, I keep in shape

I am a white woman in a green sari
    my companion, the midget, crosses and recrosses his bandy
        legs

I am the midget
    my companion wears a dot of lipstick on her brow; I adore it

I am a housewife and mother
    the midget kicks my chair, breathes on my hair

I am the breadwinner
    I carry binoculars; I have a boil on my neck

I am a teacher from Kansas
   I have run away to love, to give and receive

I am a widow, I prefer dark meat, the liver
   I sew having buried my husband's genitals

I am Christ
   everyone knows my story; I am surrounded

I am Judas
   I am cursed in bars

We are the camels, we drive Pilate the fanatic
   crazy with our filth

I am Peter, I am bored to death
   denying my Master three nights a week

I am the blind man, I switch my ball from hand to hand
   anxious for the cock to crow

I am the child
   He has promised me Eternal Life

We the the lovers
   our mouths water

I am the teacher
   crush my lips

We are the clerics
we are on vacation

I am the breadwinner
my boil has come to a head

I am the mother
I have lost a breast; my husband wipes his neck

I am the midget, I feel
spikes in my feet, I kick

I am his companion
I tried to be a Catholic

I am the son, my father says wait
your turn will come

I am the mannikin
at the Resurrection I rise, I glow

We are the hands that man the booths at the end
we hold up beads, authentic rags

We are the ones who rush
who brush away our tears, who buy

# THE LIFE OF THE WOLF

Surrounded by tigers,
pandas, and piles
of marked-down sweat-
shirts, by blown-up gnus
chewing their cuds and clerks
huddled like pocket mice,

he presses *The Life
of the Wolf* to his coat
and trembles to own it,
to have hairy feet
and impossibly keen
hearing, and to move

mainly by moonlight.
His cousins, the coyote
and kit fox, would call him
swift, and sheep
dreaming his jaws,
dreaming his rangy legs

would swoon in their fur
at his touch.
A most faithful beast,
if the right female
pricked up the hairs on his neck
he would mate forever.

For her he would tear out
the best meat, give her silver
pups to suckle, and tackle
ranchers if the moose and caribou,
the deer and elk gave out.
On rainy nights in the den

**54**

he would treat her to rhythms:
"Delicate little dik-diks
scamper on the savannah"—
and she would roll over
rubbing his side as if lost
in the ripest flesh.

Or maybe he'd fall for a collie,
and get shot forsaking safety
in the outskirts—
and she too would get shot
going for the killer's, her owner's,
throat in revenge . . .

And they'd all die out,
as in fact they were,
unable to find a place in the country,
a place away from men
riding shotgun in low-
flying planes . . .

With only their ghosts
on the shelves,
reduced and filled
with stuffing,
with fake gray fur
and satin ribbons.

# THE MAN AND THE GOSHAWK

For two straight days
around the clock, dust
has settled on their backs
and they have shared the attic,
hollow-cheeked as lovers
who can't call it off —
the man grown stiff
in some old crushed
velvet chair his mother
left behind, the hawk
in jesses, clinging to his arm.
You'd think an artist
with a taste for veiny eyes
sat them there and bellowed:
*Do not move, you're beautiful!*
—and mainly they behave.
When the man's wife
hands up live blue mice
trembling in a shoe box,
she, the hawk, barely pecks at them —
you can see
her heart's not in it.
But the man does not
lose faith; he chews
another No-Doz and goes over,
once again, the book
of kings at falconry.

The thing is: he must win
the goshawk's confidence,
must wait for her to feel
free enough to fall asleep.
By tomorrow that will happen.
Then the next day
feed her beef heart, raw
—just enough
to make her hungry;
then he'll give her twenty
feet or so of line
and let her go
and pull her in,
and let her go
and pull her in again to meat.
Let her go, he thinks,
and pull her in;
let her go
and pull her in again to meat;
let her go
and pull her in,
let her go
and pull her in
until she loves me.

# BURN-OUT

In the vacant lot
next to Eddie's Sundries, two young bruisers

forty feet apart, in heat,
burn a baseball back and forth.

Dry, I step inside
for beer,

The cooler's empty; Eddie's widow lifts her eyes
from Maeterlinck's *Life of the Bee*—

she knuckles the sweat on her lip
and calls the Hamm's man a son of a bitch.

I nod,
she lights a Kool

and sighing returns to her page.
I leave.

Outside, the boys have moved in
a dozen feet. The game is serious,

speechless, the ball lands with an oily *smack!*
It takes me back. I remember

how red my palm got
when I caught the ball too much

in the pocket
instead of the webbing—

and once so hard in the lower gut
I urinated pink for a week.

Suddenly one boy yells "You mother!"
and makes a wild heave over the other's

head. The ball hits and cracks
the plastic PEPSI sign sticking out of Eddie's.

They scram.
Eddie's widow's face

appears behind the screen
like an engraving. I can't tell how

she feels. Then
the Hamm's man

pulls his truck up, jumps down grinning.
Eddie's widow steps outside, she's wearing

yellow bedroom slippers sporting
dandelions. Shading

her tiny eyes
with the bee book, she blinks at the street,

then at the sky.
Several seasons go by.

The Hamm's man, loading his dolly,
throws her a wolfish whistle.

But she is still blinking—trying to make sure,
I think, the sky isn't kidding,

and that her eyes are in OK,
and that the voice saying

"Save it, lard ass"
really belongs to her,

and she to us, whoever we are,
before it's time to go in.

# XMAS

1. Deck the halls with git.
2. Git the halls.
3. In a gitfall, stick out your tongue.
4. Remember when gitfalls were bigger?
5. For grandmother: a warm, practical git.
6. For Bing: a white git.
7. For that man on the go: a go git.
8. Git comes in all sizes, including no-return.
9. Git is color-blind & lays down its arms.
10. Jingle git.

## MEETING MY BEST FRIEND
## FROM THE EIGHTH GRADE

He says when he comes in a bar
after beating Wyoming, say,
there's something like fur in the air
and people don't see him, they see a bear.

My best friend from the eighth grade is a coach.
He wants to Go Go Go Go—
He wants to Get There!—and gives me a punch.
His wife, in lime slacks, curls on the couch.

I ask him where
and thinking it over he pounds his palm; his eyes stare.
His wife passes peanuts, teases
his touchy hair.

He says never mind
and changes the subject to button-hooks, quick dives
—old numbers in our pimples we were famous for.
Nineteen years go by; he calls it a crime.

His wife cracks two more Buds, stretches, calls it
a night; we hear the door click.
Flushed, he flicks on the television . . .
We bend our beer cans like dummies, and sit.

# AROUND THE HORN

*New Year's Eve*

Eddie's on the mound
bearing down,
& I'm at shortstop, spitting in my pocket!
—We're the twelve-and-under champs so cocky in our jocks
it hurts . . .

God damn it Jack
that skinny kid at second's white
from drowning. Butch
in right
caught polio—they drove a nail deep
into his quick good knee
to slow the bone,

& Eddie packs a gun for blacks . . .

A little compensation, Captain,
half the field tilts . . .

Where's my girl who squirmed
in roomie's Buick
over Easter break?

My sister snug in rabbit?
—while beaming me wore Father's watch!

It's midnight
& I won't grow up—
I'm Teacher's blended pet,
crocked & cold . . .

I need sweet Judy's coat of arms,
her baby breasts . . .

That midget grinning in the hole is dead.

# THAT SUMMER

That summer at the lake
when the malemute babies
nuzzled their bones
under the cabin's floor;
when Cyrus and Meeno
stayed up late to watch
a moth weave the screen
then each other,
taking days to blink;
when the patient waves
nudged the alewives
to shore, and a startled possum
flicked his pink paws at us;
when the path we took
on our morning walk
sparkled with tracks
and our feet and knees
and then our backs
and tongues got wet
there was nothing,
not one thing
under the sun or moon
or those sweet cedar boughs
that could touch us.

# KNEELING IN THE SNOW

I pray for my uncle
who quit seeing us
beating his cancer like Tarzan,

for a woman
clawing her raw, swollen belly,
her amber tongue stuck out for dope.

I pray for my daughter beating her wings,

for my father and grandfathers
hunched like bears
under the covers,

for their women
who remember the slaughter
before the wedding.

I pray for my fear,
may we lie down together.

# THE RUNNER

## Gary Gildner

1978

# MY FATHER AFTER WORK

Putting out the candles
I think of my father asleep
on the floor beside the heat,
his work shoes side by side
on the step, his cap
capping his coat on a nail,
his socks slipping down,
and the gray hair over his ear
marked black by his pencil.

Putting out the candles
I think of winter, that quick
dark time before dinner
when he came upstairs after
shaking the furnace alive,
his cheek patched with soot,
his overalls flecked with
sawdust and snow,
and called for his pillow,
saying to wake him
when everything was ready.

Putting out the candles
I think of going away
and leaving him there,
his tanned face turning
white around the mouth,
his left hand under his head
hiding a blue nail,
the other slightly curled
at his hip, as if
the hammer had just
fallen out of it
and vanished.

**67**

# THE RUNNER

Show the runner coming through the shadows,
 show him falling into a speckled rhythm,
 and then show the full expression of light,
 there, where the trees quit and the road
 goes on alone, marked by the moon-glazed gravel

Show the runner trying to disappear
 where sky and road meet far in the distance,
 show him always a step too late,
 show a train going by hauling a long silence,
 and show the runner leaving the road
 where the killdeer starts from a charred stump

Show the runner saying the names of streams
 as if he were working off days in purgatory,
 show the Chocolay, the Rifle, the Fox,
 the Laughing Whitefish, the Escanaba,
 show the runner's pocketful of worms
 and show the runner's father
 sitting alone by a hole in the ice

Show the runner stopping at farm after farm
 until a woman appears who is wearing a child's
 pink kimono over her shoulders,
 show her feet in hunting socks
 a kitchen arranged in cream and linoleum,
 show that the wind has toasted her cheeks,
 show that she doesn't know what he wants

Show the runner's old room, the crucifix
 he tied fresh palms around each year,
 the five nice birch his father planted,
 the two blue spruce, the silver maple,
 the cherry from the nursery that was going broke,
 the man who said take it for a buck,
 the hail storm that knocked them over

Show the runner setting out all spruced up,
   show the sun, poached, above a grove of leggy birch,
   show the runner cruising down a cow path
   trying to catch his breath,
   and show the slim white limbs dividing
   letting him in

Show the runner peeling bark
   and scratching messages with sticks,
   then show him diving into a drift,
   nosing like a mole out of season,
   rolling over and over
   and yipping for luck or in pain

Show the runner approach the only light
   in Little Lake, there, over the grocer's
   fading pack of Camels,
   show the grocer chewing Red Man,
   listen to him play his pocket change
   and resurrect the dead,
   listen to him spit them back

Show the runner running on,
   show the moon, then show it stalking him
   across the road into the second growth,
   show the runner's father in his garden
   blue and out of breath and looking hard
   at something nothing can distract him from,
   show the lake all frozen over,
   show the mound of snow

# JOHANN GAERTNER (1793–1887)

In the blue winter of 1812
Johann Gaertner, a bag of bones,
followed Napoleon home.
He was cold; Napoleon,
riding ahead under a bear
wrap, fumed at the lice
in his hair. —From Moscow
to Borodino, from Borodino
to the Baltic Sea, Napoleon
fumed and slapped, and glared hard
at the gray shapes
pushing at his face.
And maybe ate a piece of fruit
he did not taste. If he
cried, we do not know it.
But Johann Gaertner, 19,
a draftee, a bag of bones,
blew on his fingers
and bit them, and kicked at his toes.
And chewed and chewed
a piece of pony gristle.
And once, trying to whistle
an old dog into his coat,
swallowed a tooth.
*God save Johann!* Johann
Gaertner, 19, cried,
moving his two blue feet
through bloody holes his eyes
kept staring and staring at . . .
And in the midst of all this
one night God appeared, hoary and fat,
and yelled at him in Russian,
*Kooshat! Kooshat!*—
and Johann closed his eyes

**70**

waiting for one of his sharp white bones
to pierce his heart.
When none did, he dragged them
past the mirror Napoleon
gazed and gazed at his rasp-
berry-colored chin in . . .
and past windy St. Helena
where his former leader was already lost
among the washed-up herring.
And Johann kept going,
no longer hearing that tooth
grinding against his ribs,
but starting to feel the sun
on the back of his neck
for a change, and loving the itch
and salty wash of sweat
everywhere on his chest.
    And one day
holding up a jug of cool switchel,
he had swig upon swig upon swig
and felt his whole blessed mouth
turn ginger—
and he whispered a song
that came out *Ah, Johann* . . .
    Thus,
having stopped, he stepped back
and took in his fields of hay,
his acres and acres of feed,
and his six black bulls
bulging against the sky.
And sitting down he ate
the giant mounds of sweet
red cabbage his ample wife

set before him,
and the pickled corn,
and the mashed potatoes dripping
galaxies of gizzards, hearts,
and juicy bits of wing,
and yet another slice
of her salt-rising bread
spread with his own
bee-sweetened butter.
(Often Johann stretched out big
in the clover, listening to his bees,
*churn, churn,* they said, *churn* . . .)
And praising God while licking his fingers
he allowed for a wedge of her
sour cream raisin pie,
and a mug of steaming
coffee out on the porch,
where he liked to stick his stockinged feet
among the fireflies,
and feel the slow closing
of his eyes . . .
          And all of this
(including the hickory-nut cake,
rhubarb wine, and the fine old fat-
bellied kitchen stove)
happened for many years
in little Festina, Iowa,—
where Anton Dvorak came to drink
local Bohemian beer
and hear the Turkey River;
and where rosy Johann Gaertner
dug down deep in the rich black dirt
to make his own hole
and one for his wife as well.

# TODAY THEY ARE ROASTING
# ROCKY NORSE

Today they are roasting Rocky Norse.
Me, today they are roasting me
while I sit here, dead from the belt down.
But hey! Look at these trousers. Black Nickle
born with a ball in his palms, Mr. Real Fine Hands,
he'd say Man those are fly pants, man. Fly.
& wiggle both flat hands down by his hams
cooling everything. Black Nickle. Who came in grim & gray
when they propped me up in all those good pillows, all that
pretty gash flashing their choppers around my head, pop, pop
ROCKY NORSE IS FIGHTING BACK. Gray, man, he was *ash*.

I like pork, always have. Smell it boys
& tell me what's better, clean sweat pants
or a woman from South Dakota—from someplace
you never heard of—keeping it warm in the parking lot.
Her old man raised sheep but she raised the moon
raised it up & gave it over. Fly, Mr. Rocky.
Or clean socks & no god damn throbbing
knees & shoulders when it rains.
I'll tell you what I liked about that woman.
She could drive all day over South Dakota
& two more hours over Minnesota
& still raise the moon soft & mellow.

I remember one time I looked in the sky over Red Oak
& he threw me a horse-wink, the grinning fool.
Another time grabbing that salamander,
it was so orange she wanted to eat it.
Pump pump went its throat. Pump pump pump.
Finally I put it down. Go on, get out of here.
Go raise some big kids that can tackle.
South Dakota said Rocky you are my man.
South Dakota said that, her & her funny dreams.

73

Somewhere water's dripping on a sink full of nylons.
Another beer? Sure, give it here. & when my baggie's full
kid you can empty it, how's that? Today is my day.
Roasting Rocky. & the Smoke going up from that hog
is going up all over the Midwest, going up over St. Cloud
Bemidji & even Dee-troit where Snake hauled his buns
out of & tore over my ass one time so quick & beautiful
nothing would ever stop him & nothing did, the greaser
safety wet his pants just straining to watch I believe.

What was that dream she had down in Dallas? God yes
she said Rocky you carried around a sack of darkness
like a sack of black dirt & you tied it next to your belly.
I said how about a sack of money honey, but she went on
those green eyes big & wide & all that red hair falling
everywhere, saying I laid down with it & stroked the folds
like I wanted it to take me in.

Wake up baby, I am here! ROCKY NORSE the sign says
& the arrow is pointing straight at that hog
I am getting the first piece of. Free.
Along with all the Hamms I can pour in my baggie.
& everyone's shown up except those two bastards
who were raised on ears & lips & parts
no one can stand to even look at.
But I guess I spook Nickle
& maybe Snake is dead. Which I can say I am glad
I am not. Hey listen. All that sponge they cut from my knees,
what difference does it make to me now?

You get used to everything. If I could do it
without spitting up all over my tie
I'd lead a cheer. OK fans

gimme ah *you!*
gimme ah *get!*
gimme ah *get-used-to-EVERYTHING!*

South Dakota swing your smooth moon up here
next to my King Daddy Seat of Honor
& tell the folks about that seed you
found on the sheet between your dimpled knees.
What'd it look like baby?
A kidney bean Rocky & it was breathing
I wanted to put it back in
but I couldn't & I couldn't
find anyone who would
I touched it Rocky
& it stopped breathing
a piece of paper, that's all it was
a piece of paper folded in half
no, I opened it up
Rocky it was a plastic sack
you were inside
all of your little pieces . . .

My first bike was a fat-tired job the Red Oak
Sears had to special order. & I know exactly
where that bike is today, it's frozen under
Crab Smoltz's hog barn. When they were all
standing around with their little pliers fixing my spine
I saw that fat-tired honey rising up shiny & new
from the wet cement I'd pushed it into, rising up

with the first good man who ever taped my ankles
glued to the seat & twisting those grips for
all he was worth, saying Rocky I got this machine
but it's too much! Take it off my hands!
So I took that shiny Red Flyer off Coker's
small swift hands & rose up past Crab Smoltz's
sun-roasted face & his hogs that looked just like him
& past my old man saying quit running
those cows when they're full god dammit
up past Snake & South Dakota up past Nickle up past
the Mayflower truck that wouldn't move & the long
white line I laid my nose against thinking this is one
godawful wrong place to fall off
my brand new Harley & cream . . .

I think when God sits back & looks
at everything he made he gets
a hole in his gut.
I broke everything—neck & legs & both cheeks.
& buried half a chopper in my tongue.
Hey God you ever feel like a jerk?
You ever feel looking down at this handsome boy
who could open up holes for semis
who's got to tickle out his own crap now—
you ever feel like calling in sick?

Religion, my old man said he had all of it
he needed in two hundred head & no TB.
My mother went when somebody croaked. & baked something.
Snake said don't knock it man.
Right baby I don't knock it, I eat pork
I eat the hog you are not here to see my name on

along with all the boys & their trim women
who cut it up in little pieces
at twenty-five bucks a plate,
along with South Dakota & her red hair
falling all over those white shoulders.

I am eating pork with a hole in my tongue
hey Snake I am going down, my juice baby
my meat are making muscle. Tearing open
those slots baby, moving everything to one side
& coming back where they don't see us
they don't see us Snake but they smell something
real good going up over Red Wing going up
over Shenandoah over Winona over Dallas & New York City
they want in baby they are screaming their guts out
they want in so bad  . . .

They want in where the water won't
quit dripping baby tell them how it is.
Tell them you are my turtle
you save my legs from the sharks.
But please don't say my heart is a peach
my heart is a bag of nuts somebody cut off
one of Crab's pigs, milky blue blood
is pumping it baby milky blue blood
tell them

# WHEN THE RETARDED SWIM

at the Y on Fridays
a lot of time is taken up
with holding them, so they do not drown.
They whoop and squeal, they sound
like children given some wine
with their bread, but their bones
will not follow smoothly
where the flesh wants them to.
The retarded enter the water like cattle,
slowly, led down a sloping gangway
by a man with a full, curly beard.
He makes them bellow—their large eyes
dart in every direction, their feet
think the water is fire, or Jello,
or something else altogether lovely.
Some of the men get erections
and thrash at toys the attendants
have set to bobbing, their pink eyes
made pinker by chlorine,
and two or three of the women
find squiggly fish in their suits
and are beside themselves with joy . . .
and no one ever wants to go.
Outside, miles away, it may be
October or the dead of winter.
Leaves clutter an old man's walk
or snow lies frozen under a sparrow's
peck and weave. Wetting a finger
the old man discovers which way
the wind wants to blow his fire,

and the sparrow suddenly flies away
toward another part of the city,
where it is summer — where a young boy,
his eager hands far too small,
bobbles a ball —

                     But he runs after it.

Seventeen of the poems in "Letters from Vicksburg" are based on a series of letters written by a Union soldier to his wife in Iowa. The man spelled pretty much by ear, often employing *t* for *d* or *s* (writing *hat* for *had*, for example, and *Divition* for *Division*), and he used no punctuation—the letters simply run on, broken up only by occasional paragraphing (here and there I have used extra spacing to indicate pauses and stops). I tried to remain faithful to this grammar, especially when a phrase like "scars of amunition"—meaning "scarce of ammunition"—occurred. The last poem is based on a letter from an officer—found with the soldier's—and I tried to keep his formality. I view these eighteen sonnets as translations, even though I did not use all of the original material and departed from it whenever it seemed necessary or fruitful.

G. G.

# LETTERS FROM VICKSBURG

### I

Aprile the 17/63

Dear woman I am well and hope you ar
the same    to tell you wher we ar will be
a mater prety hard for I dont hartly
now my self    but now the River is not far
we hav to stop and fix the leavy ther
at Carthage wher we aim the enemy
is fortifying    fifteen hundret men
we hav forty thousand here and one
hole Divition has been promised soon
they want to kep us out of Jackson Miss
if we can cut the Rebels off from ther
in Vicksburgh we will giv them holy thud
well I must hury up and finish this
the boys ar well and in good hart    John Blood

## II

### May the 7/63

Dear woman I was glat to hear from you
yours of Aprile 29 and glat
to hear that you was well and Edward to
we hav hat hart fighting sins we crost
the Missippi   many maimed and lost
a plan to martch was met by Rebels near
Port Gibson   they was in a canebrake ther
we hat to drive them out with beyonet
witch we don with fulsom sped and got them
on the open field wher we shot them
down by hundrets but they stot thair ground til
noon   they tried retreat   we charged and killed
til sunset   Captain Staley lost is sord
and I my cap for witch I thank the Lord

### III

We left the River seven days ago
with 3 days Rations   sins our battel
I hav hartly climed down from my satel
looking for a bite   2 days ago
12 miles from Camp our squat came to a nise
plantation with a grove around it and
a hedge   so that the inmates of the house
dit not notise our aprotch   when they
saw us stanting at the dore they jumped
and screamed   I told them they neat not be scart
for we was only yankey soldiers only
hungry and was never nowen to hert
the ladies   so we took posesion of
the tabel ate a harty dinner   then
helpt ourselfs to other things we wanted

## IV

Dear woman I again take pen in hand
to let you now that I am well this day
I hav nothing new to write   we stand
mutch nearer Vicksburgh in a redish clay
in a line of battel sevrel miles
up and down a creek   we heare the Rebels
plan to meat us here and meat us ther and
I dont giv a blast   sixty thousand men
stand by tonight and we expect to be
reanforsed to twise that by tomorrow
I hat ment befor to tell you that we
use the Zouave Drill   laying down to load
ther by saving many men the hollow
road   the male mule is here   goodby   John Blood

## V

May the 17/63

Dear woman I am sor a littel bit
but I will tel you some thing of our martch
to Vicksburgh yesterday    befor I quit
to sleep    the boys hav not hat mutch
we hat just come off a suny field
when they hit and cut us all to peases
I never notised the retreat at first
every thing was falling thick with dust
the men all jumped into a ditch and layed
down    and fired onse or twise    I jumped in
and fired onse or twise and looked around
to see what all the boys was doing now
being that the shooting stoped    and they was
running fast but for a few that huncked
the ground and wept as close as posable

## VI

Dear wife I feal prety rested now
and wil continue with my pen   I said
the Rebels hat us close and hot and how
I got away with all thair balls so hard
behind was I just ran   and just as I
got to the Regiment Sam Hamitt fell
hit 2 plases   thro the breast and thro the thi
he lost his head and begged for me to make him well
I dragged him to a plase of shelder
in the shade ther he was out of danger
then I wiped his fase but dont
now what he tried to say   the Rebels hat thair
guns on me   I let them hav the contents
of my own and ran   not nowing wher I went

## VII

Dear wife and friend I dozed but now will try
to finish this   I wanderd in the thick
until my hart sloed down   I hat to ty
my foot   for I hat looked and seen the slick
collecting ther along my boot   they shot
my big toe off   also I was struck
with grape against the neas   my pants wer cut
by glancing balls witch left me welds on both
my angels   God hat bilt me tall enough
I gess   I herd a halt   to my surprise
General Logan and his forse of seven
thousand stot beyond the treas   O Heaven
help the Rebels now   I hureyed up to him
and said our men wer going down like flys

## VIII

I went with General Logans men and we
confused the Rebels so they jumped around
and did not now witch end to pick    see
we hat them in a pintch    and then we made
a charge with beyonets    a few wer ful
of furie yet but Logans men wer fresh
and yeled like farm boys raising gutsie Hell
at gelding time    2,000 prisoners
we took    I helped to make them safe    one cursed
my other foot but he hat such a mess
about his ear and fase I payed no mind
I hat to go back on the Battel ground
in serch of my own Regiment    my feet
steped over deat and wounted thick as sheep

## IX

May the 27/63
at Vicksburgh

Dear wife and friend I hav not mutch to write
for it has only been a steady rore
of muskets canons mortars and just mor
of that sins the begining of our fight
on the 16th    no telling when the scrape
of shels will end or how    the Rebels ar
surroundet so they cant with lif escape
our line of battels over ten miles long
gunboats guart the River and our trench
is all the way around thair forts    a pintch
so close they cant get to thair canons
if any one will show himself we sling
the balls out after him and black him down
my love to you    my sheat has no mor room

**X**

May the 30/63
Camp near Vicksburgh

Dear loved one well the last 2 days I spent
down in the trenches    now Im out and dont
feal mutch like writing letters on account
of not mutch sleep    but I should tell you what
I mean by beaing in the trenches
I mean by beaing in the trenches that
a ditch was dug in clear around the fort
within a hundret yards of them    and that
we hav our batrees planted in the trench
behind us throwing shels up in thair fort
all the time we throw the shels in    in fact
they must be getting scars of amunition
for I hav not heart over 3 reports
from them sins I am in my station

## XI

Dear loved one did I mention General Grants
trik he pulled on Rebel General Johnston
when we captured Jackson    well he sents
a telegraph    sent him amunition
quik    for them Damd yankeys ar acomin
then he sined it with the Rebel Generals name
when the train pulled into Edwarts station
loaded down with shels and canon balls we
captured it    so I think thair artilry
is about played out    I may be rong    jokes
can turn against you    but I hope its true
weve only lost 4 men sins coming heare
2 of them by bad shels from our own
I sent my love to you and all your folks

⁂

## XII

Dear wife and bosom friend I hat seen hart
sites before I ever saw a battel
field    at Edwarts station hospitel
I fount out what it was to see a hert
the one that makes me dry hat lost his tong
the ball past thro his teeth and cut it off
and made his eyes and everything look rong
but heare theres times with the secesh thats grate
we dont shoot at them after dark and they
of corse dont shoot at us   the moon shines so
that we can see each other plain as day
we hav the right to go half ways acrost
and they can come half ways acrost to us
we leave our arms and some come cleare acrost

## XIII

June the 6/63
Camp SE of Vicksburgh

Dear Cecelia well its shel and shel and
welcom more deserters evry night   they
tell us they get just a litel corn bread
and thair amunitions low   I can say
another thing   that when the win blows on us
from that way we cant stay put   because it
stinks so bat   no ones hert and 2 ar sick
the Lutenant has the peevish diaree
the Sergent has Consumption and the flux
well I dont now whi you dont write to me
I hav to write and do write evry chance
I get   I dont now wether you dont write
or wether I dont get them in this plase

## XIV

June the 12/63
Camp rear of Vicksburgh

Dear Cecelia we hav hat some warm times
in the Company sins last I wrote to you
on Monday the Lutenant died    and Sims
first Corprel died of feaver    and a slew
of other vakancys ar coming up
as officers receive paroll    the way
we fil them is by vote    well the question
of Lutenant laid between Lon Baily
and myself    only Colonel Connell hat
promised Baily and he fount out if he
left it to the vote whi I would get three
forth    so he sent rite strate for Bailys bars
now he wants to make me sargent    well heres
what I want    nothing    if it aint by vote

## XV

Some boys ar playing cards but I dont feal
like it    it is a prety night altho
the stink is bat    to bat the win cant blow
the other way    or rain a bit and peal
off thair scud    they hav horses mules and cows
runing round thair forts and when they get to
neare we shoot them    dogs or anything    a sows
thair now that they could surely put to
use    but it wont help a thing except I
gess the ground    and this grounds rich enough
talk is they hav hopes of General Johnston
coming in our rear to help them out    rough
chance of that    in the mean time if they try
to bury aney stinking corps we shoot them

## XVI

July the 24/63
Millikens Bend La

Dear and most Loved wife it is with pleasure
I sit up to write you    but I cant say
I am well this time    I hav hat Chill feaver
ever sins I wrote you last    yesterday
I did not have it    or today yet    plus
I am in hopes I hav it broke    dear mate
I hope this finds you well and Eddie to
I have not hat a singel letter from you
for a month    o you dont now how    anctious
I can feal    one come to the 28th
and my brother sent it on to Vicksburgh
but the man he sent it by he never
gave it to me    it is lost    and aney
way I gess hes gone with Grant to Georgy

## XVII

July the 31/63
Millinkens Bend La

Dear and Mutch Loved One with pleasure I take
my pen and opertunity to let
you now Im still among the living but
not well   I hat Chill feaver   hat that broke
then took a bat dyree witch I cant stop
all the metacen dont seem to help
it only helps to weaken me to sor
but I would like so mutch to now whi I
dont get a letter from you aney mor
if you decitet you dont want to write
me aney mor just let me now   be shore
to anser this one soon   if in a short
time I dont heal I shal try to land
a furlow and come home   goodby   John Blood

## XVIII

Berwick La.
Oct 2nd 1863

Mrs. Blood. Dear Madam, Yours of Sept. 13
arrived to hand last night. I must be mean.
We had for some time previous no word
from your good husband, one of Iowa's
brave sons. Then we had the word that he was
coming back. As time went on no further word
from John until a week ago we heard
that he had died aboard the "R. C. Wood"
of Typhoid fever August 4. I have sent
his final statements and his military
history on to Washington D. C. Truly
I assure you, Madam, I was hurt,
for John was hardy, in the best of health —
but O alas! in life we are in death.

# THE PAGE TURNER

Anonymous, she takes her chair
beside the bench on which the French
piano player sits, arranging his hands.
She wears a yellow dress,
and her face is flushed the color
love composes, waiting for him,
and the flutist, to begin.
Her own hands hold each other.
Then the world, wakened,
hears its first bright noises —
leaning forward she is quick to follow:
they are on a river riding over shallows,
over morning mist toward its source.
Each time she turns a page
she feels a minnow brush her fingertips.
But here is where the world starts
to take her, where the river narrows
to a rapids — here
among the flecks of sunlight bouncing
off the rocks, off the backs of flickers diving
past her shoulders, off the leaves
gathered, swirling, in a pool.
She is all alone and doesn't know it —
doesn't know her body's free,
nor that she's found the falls
the flutist moving faster almost dancing
and the French piano player in his madness
to control the birds his hands have turned into
have given her, alone, among a thousand nervous witnesses.
Nor later when she tries to sleep beyond her tears
will she know that joy applauds
and loves her for her frailty.

# 4th BASE

Decked out in flannels and gripping my mitt
I was running laps, long grassy laps,
and hearing my 200 bones start to chatter—
I had finally arrived in the major leagues!

I stopped in the infield, dropping
to a shoulder stand—my big toes pointing out the sun!—
and there was no pain, even at 37.

Then we started to play—I was at 4th—
and my first throw over to 1st
bounced in on the 10th or 11th dribble.

Odd, I thought,
that the game had developed such wrinkles.
But shuck that, I was here now, bounding
around my sack like a well-oiled seal, barking
"Dust everyone off! Dust everyone off!"

After a while I slipped into Mass
and sat with my old teammates—
the ones from high school who had grown pink
and jowly, and who played with their keys
between their knees, and who
when the choir leaned forward to sing our song
covered their eyes, and mumbled, and wouldn't look at me.

# THE HIGH-CLASS BANANAS

The bananas down at the Safeway
were doing OK last week, just as
they'd been doing all along probably,
just lying around on the wood bench
waiting for folks to come by &
look over what they'd like sliced up
on their Grape Nuts in the morning,
or in their raspberry Jello at night,
or maybe what they'd go for after school, plain,
with a big glass of nice cold sweet milk
—to get away from questions like
"How many lights are now on in the 1st place?"
or that other devil, "The fountain pen
was invented 1 century and 1 year
after the balloon. In what year
was the fountain pen invented?"
No, nobody had a lot of grief
over the bananas down at the Safeway,
not the way they just lay there
waiting for you, wanting to make you feel good.
Then somebody, maybe somebody who *knew*
how many lights were now on in the 1st place,
got to thinking, Hey!
why don't we get a merry-go-round
down at the Safeway? A big red carousel
that makes a little pizzaz? a little hubba hubba?
& put the bananas on it! & stick some plastic
leaves on top! & some fuzzy monkeys!
& some palm trees! & everybody pushed up close
said Yeah! They said Yeah! Yeah!
& so now we got high-class bananas
going round & round down at the Safeway.
& you stand there, maybe scratching where it itches,
waiting for your bunch to come around.

# LIFE & DEATH IN SKOKIE

However it began, it began almost at once—

He would dress her up like a little Greenland doll
   & kiss the insides of her elbows,
   the tops of her knees
   & then, as if lost in a howling storm,
   drift into sleep.

She would find notes he had left marking his place
   in adventure stories, books he would never finish;
   always they said, "I have never sizzled."

He would stand in a cold telephone booth, his wisdom
   tooth aching, & listen to her hum.

She would follow him to a bar in a foreign neighborhood
   & while he sat in the back under a rack of antlers
   she would slip down beside his tires
   & let all the air out.

He would bump her begonia off the antique whatnot,
   scuff his loafers in the dirt,
   then make tracks for the club
   where he worked on his old windup
   & practiced approaching the net.

She would draw his funny bone in charcoal
   then rub it, ferociously, until her cheeks burned.

He would eat a celery stick
   & slap the latest averages.

She would read the life of Edward Hopper, the life
   of Kierkegaard, the life of Fanny Brice,
   & crack Brazil nuts, almonds, or chew ice.

He would open his eyes in the middle of the night
& declare he only wanted a mountain life,
declare he only wanted to raise goats & have a wife
wake him up nights when mice scrapped in the rafters.

She would promise to can his pumpkins.

He would promise to churn the earth.

She would say, "But something else is trying to surface . . ."

He would say, "But something else is trying to roll free . . ."

# STATISTICS

*"They say that couples who've been married five years don't talk to
each other more than twenty-seven minutes a week."*—overheard

Statistics say the heart is a long-stemmed glass
    you happen across after the party has busted up,
    that red wine crusted over the lip the kiss
    you once felt down to your toes, down where
    the minnows poured themselves into a giant silver drop

Statistics say we are sprouting stiff black bristles
    in all the places where we used to blush

Statistics say you will break six geranium pots
    in the seventh year, on the morning of the eighth
    you will catch yourself boring a hole
    above the old one, the one that never filled up
    standing on slivers of wishbones

Statistics say the bears in the zoo
    scratch and yawn but they won't sleep with you

Statistics say no matter how many bottles you toss in the water,
    no matter how many loops you scoop, the milkpods you puffed
    out your cheeks for, flying and flying,
    are gone, along with the grandpas
    pulling the covers up over their chins

Statistics say you will quit walking barefoot
    the summer your name disappears from the sand

Statistics say please or listen once too often
    and then they forget and say it again,
    and we always hear them, that's the wonderful part,
    and then we forget and they repeat it, slowly,
    only we are bending closer to the mirror by now
    arranging something we want just so

**104**

# LAST ARTICLES

Here is his coat;
hang it up
for the crows,
its histories
all have the same name:
wanting sun,
wanting rain.

Here the shirt,
its finest sweat
has turned into bright
pockets of heart-salt.
Hand it down
to an only son.

Here the pants—
there is a braggart inside
who could never help it.
Tear them into rags
to dust the piano,
the clock.

Finally the shoes,
those sad dependable cows
who traveled the same path
day after day
and said nothing.
Put them out in the orchard
where sparrows play.

# TOADS IN THE GREENHOUSE

When the scale were sucking
the life from my orchids,
I imported hundreds
of ladybugs into my life,—
blessing their tickle
among the sobered,
applauding the sparkle
they rendered to wrinkle
and droop. But soon these
ladies were snapped
away by the quick
sticky tongues of my toads,
whom I also had
affection for.
        Stuck,
I had to keep the leaves
breathing myself, washing
them off with soap and water,—
telling the toads when they
lumbered over to squat and watch
that what they saw was
what they saw. As always their faces
said: *We are simply here—two beauties*
*in a world gone buggy.*
And so they continued to lumber over,
keeping their mugs at the ready.

Summer began to steady itself
against autumn, my strongest spider
moved slower and slower
up in her corner, the ants
seemed to have scrammed for good.
Only the sluggish and slimy slugs,
I thought, kept the toads going.

I started leaving angleworms out
on a piece of musty pine
they liked, making sure
the worms were lively.
*These little squiggles,* they replied,
*are adequate.*
                    Every night they'd
either be perched on the pine,
waiting, or hopping toward it.
I saw they were losing
their skins, scratching at the tough
places it wouldn't come off.
Then one night in a dream
they revealed themselves as uncles,
a wee bit hung over:
*honey bees,* they gargled,
*bring us honey bees.*
I ran toward them, my hands
brimming with mud, my feet freezing.
*No,* they said; *the sweetness,*
*the sweetness . . .*

In the morning frost had come—
and in the greenhouse, each to a pot,
the toads had burrowed down
among the roots;
I saw their noses briefly—
and then like deliberate
wonderful fish,
like prairie dogs,
or like uncles who can't quit
chasing the ladies,
they were gone.

**107**

# POEM

My daughter and I lie in the snow
    beating our wings
  and making breath—the sky
    slings it away.

Underneath, she says, is summer,
    underneath are all the fish
  and cricket bones
    and where we go to die.

Once, I remembered, I captured
    three minnows
  and kept them hid in Dixie Cups
    until they froze.

Later I tucked them under my pillow
    like teeth,
  praying to God for a penny each.
    —Spiders sleep

all winter, too, she says,
    and bears in holes
  and nobody knows
    where to find them.

A bouncing dog caught by the Union Pacific
comes back.
And my Uncle Stanley who quit
seeing us

beating his cancer like Tarzan.
And a woman
squeezing her eyes in the City of Angels,
her amber tongue

stuck out for dope. —If I ever
walked across the sky,
she says, I would grab a branch.
If I ever walked across the sky.

We stop . . . and watch our breath.
The sky slings it away.
Later we look
for a new patch of snow.

# New Poems

# BLUE LIKE THE HEAVENS

Who is that boy making his slow way among
the tufts of spun sugar blooming in the timothy,
in the moon-whitened weeds by the Merry-
go-Round? And who is that slight girl
freed by the booth of wooden minnows,
her Day-Glo-painted, bitten nails
burning in his hand? Under a summer
sky-deep and still enough
to know what it means without help,
under the last bright sky of summer, tongue-tied,
my heart caught in my mouth like a live bait,
I watch them come together, and walk, and pretend
to separate — leaving behind the wheels
and dice and the woman who swallowed fire,
leaving behind the parish ladies in the silt
light of the quiet bingo tent, and the man
coming to at the edge of the parking lot,
and the moon-hard windows of the boy's school
across the way — until they are out of sight.

Where did they go, finally?
Idaho? Arkansas? The glades of Florida?
(The girl had mentioned these places.) Back
so far into history they had to learn Latin?
(The boy had told of stumbling after Caesar's parts
of Gaul with Sister Ambrozine.) Once, at sunset,
passing through Santa Fe on the train, I thought
for a few real seconds I had seen them leaping
from a trestle, grinning, as if they had just got away
with something. But when I blinked and looked again
it was only me, my red face in the window.

I had last seen them under the bubbled roof
of the stilled Tilt-a-Whirl, listening to a cricket.
And for a long while the cricket sang their song,
as crickets sometimes did in the old days,
and the heavens rose and fell in a sweet, confusing,
terrible way, and the boy kissed her lips
—which were like . . . like nothing he had ever tasted.
But if you insisted he describe their taste,
and promised not to make fun of him,
being a boy he would say blue, like the heavens.
And all the while the cricket continued
to sing their song . . . and the boy believed
he would soon burst and scatter like a star.
But then something strange happened: the girl raised
one of her legs, and with a fingertip painfully chewed
back to where the kernel of Day-Glo polish began,
she carefully traced the scar the Fabulous Marvin's
capybara flicked on her thigh in Dallas
—and traced it again and again, pushing down hard
at the raw trail until it turned almost white,
and finally, when it came back ribbed and raw forever,
she whispered, "It's the biggest rat there is."

In all the silence that followed, I was there,
wanting to say something, distract them,
help them out—anything. But I too looked away—
toward the parking lot, and the moon-hard windows
of the school, and the silt light spilling out
from the quiet bingo tent, where the parish ladies
who sold their jellies in the swirling colored
rays of The Whip were sipping final cups of coffee.
And when I looked back again they were gone—
and nothing remained but the cricket's ordinary song.

The following summer neither one was at the festival,
and in that place where she had floated
wooden fish in a tin trough for him to dip
his hand, again and again, for the silver star
and the biggest animal, a man lay on his back
and using just his mouth, kept ten or a hundred
sparkling balls aloft, and I and the children
held our breath.

# THE PORCH

Sometimes it happens
I am having a good time
just sitting on the porch
in my big brown rocker
watching the sky sneak by.

Maybe smelling the dirt
I had turned over and raked
clean for my beans
a while ago, my body feeling
used and grateful.

Or maybe recalling a long spidery
girl I had clambered up
the sand dunes with
in Michigan once, her shoulders softly
freckled by the sun.

And maybe beyond the geranium,
perched in the wild
black raspberry patch
its mother pushed it into,
there's a young speckled robin,

fat and crabby-
looking, looking
and rocking
a little,
same as me.

Sometimes it happens
the retired gentleman
across the alley will slip
into his old
green Mercury,

tip the snappy red lid
to the back of his head,
and listen to her
purr
for a spell.

And sometimes it happens
while I'm rocking here
feeling used and lucky
and happy in my juices,
that nothing happens—

the sycamores stand,
the shade does its usual
slow business
with the leaves
over my bare toes,

and easily,
oh how easily
I fall asleep
and dream of
almost touching you.

# IN THE BEGINNING

In the beginning before the boy,
before the boy and the minnowing church
and the songs they sang over the rippled pews,
in the beginning she was a check-out girl, a shy
puller of frozen beans, of bags of oranges
shaken green from their small grips and driven
north to her purple fingers. Often, then,
the seasons were only different prices
whose violet colors found her face.
*Me,* the violet smears would whisper, *me.*

In the beginning before the girl,
before the girl and the mouse in the pulpit
who scratched and scratched when their singing rose,
in the beginning he kept tabs on death
and dying up in his crib, a student actuary
with his breviary of ledgers and a spray
of ballpoints fastened over his heart.
Often, then, the world said *today* and *tomorrow.*
Often, then, the weather was an act of God.
Often, then, the seasons were neither here nor there.

In the beginning before the boy,
before the girl and the darkness they swallowed
moving past statues holding their arms out,
in the beginning the world said *you* and *this*.
Often, then, the weather was only Moon
or a skinny cousin, Canoe; and though
neither could sing they could hold on tight
when his heart was loose, or could listen close
when Cricket came and rubbed her back, back
to the creek whose waters touched her and touched her.

In the beginning before the girl,
before the boy and the minnowing church
and the salt they kissed among no one alive,
and the waters they touched and were touched by
holding on tight and listening close,
and the darkness they swallowed,
in the beginning the world said *mine.*
And the mouse lay down and was quiet.
And Cricket crawled off and was quiet.
And the world was still where they held it.

## ALWAYS IN LATE SUMMER NOW,
## IN THE CITY

I think of how the gulls hang
lightly over the lake's edge,
and how a small perch slips to the surface, tiger-striped,
and how the white birch, in places, can look at you all day
— and I think of pushing away
from the dock, pulling forward into the farther dark,
the line of pine and fir on the far shore black,
a cut moon, a few stars to lighten my cupped hands,
wondering what's under my heart
that could take me deeper.

# THE DAY BEFORE THANKSGIVING,
# A CALL COMES TO ME
# CONCERNING INSULATION

It was a woman's voice, Russian or Czech
around the edges, timid in the way
of one who needs directions in a foreign city—
"Pardon me, sir, I am calling to you
about the coming of the cold"—
and she held out her hand, I could see that,
could see it was raw and trembling
and had traveled many years without a flower.
Now we were meeting under a brutal sky,
a sky with a cold shoulder, just the two of us,
and she carried great fear for my warmth and happiness.
How could I tell her the one I loved was jolly,
had a dimple in her chin, and waited only
moments away—always moments away—
in a room prepared for us with candles and sweet breads?
"Does the snow," she said, "make blankets?
Does the ice smear the windows and stiffen your bones?"
How could I tell her my days were often foggy fields
in which even the pheasant shivered and the dog was lost?
Would she understand I spent all morning trying
to breathe like a wolverine in the clearest light,
following something driven, something crooning
in a kind of bastard French across the top of the world?
Would she give me her poor hand knowing I might
lie down beside the trap, among the trash-marks, and chew it?
"Are your children safe? Your loved ones?" she said.
Oh dear lady beyond these cold hands,
nothing is safe in my presence. I am a small hog
with a sore throat. A frog, the last egg
from the nest of a swan, even the puny squeal
of a porcupine—I will steal anything for a song.
Even your own timid voice, dear lady,
lost at the other end for a way to make me warm.

# ICE SHANTIES

Summers they sit among pine trees,
behind filling stations
surrounded by empty oil drums,
beside dog houses, chicken coops,
and sometimes you will find one
way back where the creek slides
by a swamp, lying face up, a place for
turtles to sun themselves on.

Sometimes on a cool afternoon
in early autumn, an old man
will enter one, one newly painted
with his name and address
and maybe an eagle fixed
neatly over the door,
and inside a crackling roar
coming all the way up from Detroit
as the Tigers stage a rally.

Two, maybe three more months
and he will be on the ice,
the small Coleman in the corner
keeping his coffee hot,
his hands warm, and the fresh
hole between his legs
will shine a clear cold green
light into his face,
a white-green you never see
anywhere else except near the root
end of a piece of grass.

Two, maybe three more months
and he will be up early one morning,
following his breath blossoming out
against the dark far shore,
walking in powder, over crust
and through drift, toward this place
the Tigers are now leaving
their runners stranded in,
with only one more inning to go
and nobody coming up who can save them.

Two, maybe three more months
and the grass between his legs
will be covered with snow, but he will not
be there, and the wind, adding more,
will not touch him.

# A FIELD MOUSE AT MY FISHING HOLE

He came across the ice
as if he were asleep,
and came up to my hole
and sat, his whole shivering
shape no more than one
quick thought for hawk or owl,
a spurt, a morning's circling,
an evening under stars.
He must have traveled out
in someone's shanty.
                              Now
lost in all that frozen space
he let me pick him up and
look into his face.
It was a girl's face,
I thought, hated by the yelling
jealous step-mother, whose own
had wens and wrinkles
instead of such fine whiskers
wearing a single crystal of ice.
I could see my lips reflected there,
and the blue sun, and I could see back
to the billowy nun who screeched
reaching in the closet,
dancing around with her fist
full of the Renaissance
Masters I couldn't
memorize fast enough
(once I thought her bony
index finger the figure
fixed to the crucifix).

But only some of this
had much to do with being
small and lost and hungry
in a foreign place. I laid
a minnow in my palm
and watched him eat.
                    Later
when I put him down
he chose to stay,
sitting close beside my hole
until I'd had enough
of catching nothing,
then saw where I was walking
and ran on fast ahead.

# POEM WITH LEVELS OF MEANING

Here is the first level, the high ground
you have been looking for all day.
Notice the view, the dust, and the elephant.
Notice the elephant is Asian, the easier trained,
and how the ivy, gone mad, dribbles into the cat's tray.
Notice the cat's frozen snarl, the elephant's chipped trunk,
and notice the gap in the redhead's teeth, her laugh;
clearly she's the one who plays around.

The second level gets into your skin
and sometimes rushes past that, sylphlike,
to little that adds up; ignore the beauty marks
but pay attention, for mood, to the cold sky
and that shadow that looks like a monk.
You've never been happy with this level:
the grounds are always the same shaven brown
and the redhead, despite her gappy grin, plays to win.

Now you get lucky or lost or both.
Down here it's dark but it feels so good,
and if you doze off, which is likely, you'll be soothed
by dreams of neat whiskey and new warm bread.
Remember that rainy fall day, how you stood
together waiting for someone to guess?
Nobody did, of course, that wasn't the point.
You were in love, wet clear through, and traveling south.

# UNCLE GEORGE AT THE HOME

"Uncle George says, 'My brain is eighty-two and free
and the river smells like the river, but my hands and feet,
look at them.' Uncle George says, 'Keep me company,

linoleum'—and it's linoleum all right, but no sweet
pickle and milk, no pepper, no good black
dirt to break, no boots to bend over aching

that swell ache, no crickets under the covers.
Uncle George says, 'That Sister came from Missouri.'
I came from Missouri. I watch her scurry down the hall

furry like a funnel tornado come down, bouncing,
driving straw like tenpennies into perfectly stubborn
knots no real nail could budge and I think,

'I watch her scurry down the hall furry'
and so forth, and then I know something. I know if
she was a mule I'd rub my hand on her ribs,

fingers sliding up against the grain, raising ripples
of shivers all along that backbone
and make her notice my dos-a-dos . . .

Some days I think she's a mule so much I shake. I shake
anyway but that is not what I mean, what I mean
would carry me outside by the river, where I'd wash up

slick as I need to, watching that one eye
watch me and have a chance
if I had a chance."

# ALL HALLOWS' EVE IN KANSAS

Two crows, criss-crossing, carom
over the yellow line, pulling the whiskey-
colored Kansas fields closer: loaves of weather-
beaten hay, a tile silo smiling several missing
teeth, an old rake. It

is morning, darling, did you sleep
all right? All night your new cat
cried outside the door, and a faucet
in the bathroom dropped its drips in
hiccups down the drain. Or

did you dream again your dream
of rooms, your former husband stuffing
apples in your pantyhose, and you
couldn't find and stop him? This
train of thought is wrong, as

turned around as we are, looking for the Full
Faith Church construction site, to inspect its plumbing.
Your hard hat's in the back, riding on my
tennis racquet, and your pretty eyes are raw
from last night's cattle show. Buddy

Smith, of Huntsville, Texas, forked up
straw and spat beside his sleek, hump-backed
champion Brahma, talking eggs and sperm
and body weight until you couldn't breathe
for all the dust. We

left and filled our bellies with fillet. Later,
in the room you've walled with sharks and marlin
mouthing tackle from a fling in Mexico, you cast
my stars and planets, finding Saturn
swooning, Pluto bright, or

maybe the reverse; I couldn't follow,
following the furrows in your brow, the cat
clutching at your breast, the sober fix
	with which you searched the future as it
	dipped and swirled, sat

still, played out line, and made you bite
your lip. You bite it now, wondering where
we are. Olathe, says a sign. We stop to ask
	directions at the Baptist church. A burst
	of children wrapped in sheets, sacks

to put their sweets in flapping at us, billows
past, trailed by the breathless chaperone, who waves
a ring of glistening foil, crying, "Stephanie!
	You left your halo on the milk machine!"
	Last night, bubbled in the tub, we turned

the pages of your wedding book—you wanted
me to see you had your father's nose. I saw
the Virgin hand St. Dominic the rosary, the star
	above his head, St. Catherine and her crown
	of thorns, the faithful dog, a stick

of fire in its mouth. Italian art in Kansas.
We scrubbed each other's backs, went to bed, and watched
the stars hold still. This morning, soon, I will see you
	make your sure way among the copper pipes and elbows
	at the building site, then catch my bus.

# JABÓN

Each morning when Carmina's crippled rooster
from the washtub calls the sun safely
down the mountain once again,
and the pimpled, liver-colored tower of the church
turns golden, like his favorite chicken,
Jabón puts out one red hand, nails up, and,
conducting like the cura when he came to touch his father's
eyes and mouth and hold the old woman's head, blesses, here,
his yellow pail and, there, the first of his dirty taxis.

The children on the way to school, scrubbed and sober
in their blue, emblazoned sweaters, seldom notice
Jabón any more, or say he's only the old woolmaker's
loco son—for he is working, earning money,
filling his bright yellow pail with water under
the jacaranda trees in the *jardín*, blessing the wide face
that rises to his thumbs, the leaves laureled
around his hair, the sparkling spots of sunlight
cupped in his hands and rolling through his fingers.

When Carmina's crippled rooster quits the washtub,
satisfied the sun will stay, Jabón lays the first black
rubber floormats on the sidewalk, in the warmth,
to bless and scrub the small pieces of the mountain
off, and bless again, for Mario, who is always early,
smoking his cigar. *Fuego . . . fuego,* Jabón croons,
bending over the hood, watching his teeth shine, *fuego . . . fuego,*

feeling Mario's Bleeding Heart warm beside his ear
inside the car, *fuego* . . . *fuego* . . .
All day the taxis stop for Jabón and his yellow pail,
and all day, squeezing more of the mountain
out of his good white rag, and rubbing
for his face to smile back, he sees, also,
one who stands among the jacaranda making trees on paper,
and the old woman on her hands and knees again, crawling up
the long steps toward the church's portal (like an old sow,
she is to Jabón, like a beetle, like a tick fat with blood,
and he rubs and rubs the taxi's door to make her move along)—

and all the others who appear beside his face,
sleeping, spitting on their shoes, slowly picking the strings
of pulp from their peeled oranges, laughing, waving
their hands at the wild black cloud of screeching birds
which suddenly fills the sky above the Square—
for it is early evening now, and they have risen to chase
the sun down behind the tower, to chase the old beetle out,
and to rush back and tremble the jacaranda leaves, and receive
their blessing from Jabón, who trembels and screeches with them.

# IN THE SOCIAL SECURITY OFFICE

A widow rises
and steps forward as if called upon
to say her sums—
her legs are blue as plums,
the knuckles on her handbag shine.

# A LETTER FROM MY GOOD HAND

Whenever it rains the four fingers
of my left hand lose themselves
in a sharp confusion of stars, and the ring
my husband gave me flies burning
deep into my ankle.
                                    And I hear myself
screaming to make them come back:
but the bright blood pumping into my neighbor's
perfect hedge where I kneel
tells me goodbye, and I realize
—it comes to me as clearly as the caught
notes of a bird's song while riding in the country—
I can only count to six again.
Oh please don't make me stand up
in front of the class and recite!
—and yet, there I was, thirty-five,
calling the whole street to come quick
come help me look for my fingers
under the bright stars of my neighbor's hedge.

One night I dreamt they were leaping
like salmon among the dandelions,
the last two which I sucked as a child
wanting my mouth, and waking up, reaching out
with their purple roots, moaning,
I touched my husband's face.
My husband has the face of a child,
the face of an uncle who tried to find gold
in Colorado, sleeping under the stars with his mule.
Once he said he kicked the mule, and wept,
and then my mother, reading the letter, wept too,
and I cried with her, not knowing why.

But later I understood: he was a fool,
a dreamer, and nothing he touched was worth it,
except maybe the mule, who outlived him.
My husband, a kind, intelligent man,
wakes up early and reads. He reads and smokes,
and when I point out that my ankle has two small stars
he touches me there.
                              "I don't ever want the stars
to go away," I say. And yet, one night, he cut them down.
I saw their leaves in the first grainy light, wet with rain,
scattered about my feet and clinging to the fringe of my gown.

What I fear most is drowning, and being unable to cup
the water with both hands under a pump in spring
when I love things more than I understand
and forget—for just that instant—how I am.

I am a woman with two green thumbs
and a sky full of purple martins.
They feed their babies above my asparagus spears
and do not mind my cooing and pruning.
They loop the sun, and dive, clearing the air—
and sometimes I take off my shirt and lie deeply back
in the long grass at the garden's edge,
wanting to start all over, pull a worm to my cheek
and say something witty, intelligent.
But when he takes my hand, kissing the blue
stubs and rubbing my breasts, I feel nothing
—the same nothing I felt when I reached for the branch
caught by the roaring mower, and was pulled under.

We live in a house like all the others on this street,
nice houses with good lawns, and beyond the gardens
most of us keep, children fish in the pond for bluegills.
A week ago I caught dinner; the cat that's going
blind, Illona, sat beside me washing herself.
Not thinking I said, "My grandmother got so fat
the doctor had to cut off her wedding band." Angry,
my husband left the table, and the two small bluegills lay
curled up in their grease till morning, when I ate them.

My mother's small white hands collected stones
—her favorite Petoskey looked like a turtle
and once I borrowed it and lost it.
She also collected stamps until the Navy sent
my father home for good, to carve his ducks.
At dinner no one spoke—we listened to the radio.
But one summer an old crony surprised him,
a large man with a swirling red beard who stamped
his boots in my father's shavings, and reaching out
he picked me up and swung me around,
his green eyes flashing above my father who sat
swinging his chisel and making my mother giggle.
"Do that for me," I said as I knelt in the rain
pushing the cut stars away from my feet,
"do that, do that"—
                        because I wanted to bury
my hands all the way in, deep in that stranger's
rich red beard, and hold him, and make him come back.

## "IS MY HEART REALLY BIG AS MY FIST?"

My daughter wants to know,
turning it over and over,
trying hard to hear
each pink knuckle
touching her ear.

# WHEAT

Alone up north, soaking this nutty bulgur for supper
I think of wheat and the landscapes of wheat
the furred winter, the hard-kerneled durum, the Turkey
Red smuggled over in the fierce pockets of Mennonites
of einkorn, emmer, and spelt, the ancients on the calendar
near Grandma's moony pie crusts cooling in the window
and her hot biscuits, a spoonful of butter
oozing creamily over their soft loamy interiors

Of whiskey and beer and my Polish uncles, flushed
and tanned on leave from the Army, establishing order
and chaos around the kitchen table, wanting to know
"How many fingers?" and hoisting, toasting, "Na zdrowie!"
I think of China and Kansas and Russia
of standing beside a gravel road near everything, near
nothing but rain and wheat and two Appaloosas
all leaning the same wet way

I think of school, of handing over my pickle
and braunschweiger sandwich to the big blond boxer
that stood between me and St. Joseph's, long strings of saliva
hanging down from his bubbled lips, and leaping back, sprawling
watching the sky sneak by under the Common Witch-Hazel, lying
belly down on the log bridge over Grandpa's creek, leaning
way over watching my mouth above the swarming shiners
trying to shout "Psia Krew!" like he did when the bull

Got stubborn or the cow kicked over the milk, learning years
later it meant "Dog's Blood!" and wondering why *that*
made Grandma cross herself, wondering what the shiny pink

lump was on the neck of the old farmer kneeling bent
and nut-wrinkled in the front pew of their little Standish church
*An egg,* Grandma whispered, and I believed her, remembering
the raw potato Grandpa carried in his pocket to help
loosen his stiff leg, but wondering how he got it

Under his skin like that, I think of cutting open a cock's belly
and finding the mush of wheat mixed with buckshot
of nest and nide and nye which collect pheasants
of cast and cete and mute which collect hawks, badgers, and
    hounds
of leash which collects foxes
of all the ragtail information I've collected
that will never make me rich
of the woolly itch on the back of my neck

From the scapular Grandma gave me, the Holy Family patch
at one end, the Bleeding Heart at the other, one of them dangling
past my belt and getting in the way when I had to pee fast
my back and belly prickly with hay and sweat
of running plenty ahead of
Grandpa and Prince and Nelly and the hay cutter
my shins red and sore from kicking the cut stems
following beside the unmowed edge with my burlap bag flying

Jumping over mice and garter snakes all snipped up
in the cutter's wake, over the sudden bright scatterings
of new-born rabbits I didn't catch and run with to the sweet
bee-stippled orchard, among the windfallen Goldens, the spongy
snows, and release, I think of the cold sweaty jar
of spring water waiting in the shade, of lifting it
with both hands to my mouth, inhaling aromas
of iron and cellar and wet gravel scooped

Fresh from the stream bed, of wishing
I had a mustache sparkling with drops of this water
to wipe with the back of my wrist, of pulling off the salt-
slick harnesses and slapping the horses' shoulders and flanks
letting my hand linger on their foamy hind quarters
of cantering easily beside them down to the trout's black pool
the fine hairs on my face flat on the water collecting bubbles
my muzzle in deep, like theirs, for a long drink

I think of swinging down from the barn's full mow, the rope
burning my palms, the fork overhead with its three prongs
long as a man's arm tight against the pulley, descending
through dust- and feather-flecked sheets of fading light
and hearing my young uncle howling from the roof of the granary
hearing a late killdeer's last noisy shriek and hearing
my uncle again under the close and giddy first star of evening
howling he was stone blind gone to hell drunk on wheat wine
and what did the damn pigs and chickens and cows, what did
    the damn bull think of that

# IT'S SPRING, LOVER

Look, our farmer friend is finally
shaking out his winter
underwear—
and there's your nylon
kicking on the willow branch!

# OLD FARM IN NORTHERN MICHIGAN

Barn, you have leaned too far
trying for those wormy apples.
Now your cows will never come back
and fill their pails with cream.
Now the horse will never come back
with its hot breath and sweaty collar.
Barn, you have leaned too far—
even the cat thinks you are crazy
and stays close to the car.

# A MEMORY

My father's corn is knee-high for the Fourth
and his left side is stronger,
but he hasn't whipped
the grass into shape
and he broods
about a brassy hen pheasant
that flutters into his dreams
to nest on his heart.
He likes her,
he likes her better than all those
damn pills the doctor makes him buy!
Twice one night she got him up
but that's all right—
he ate cereal in the moonlight,
and walked in the long grass, drifting back
to his father's farm.
There was new snow on the ground
and Brownie, the collie, lay covered with it.
Barefoot
he went out
and reached under
to feel her, to make sure she was breathing,
and to say, Come to bed,
I have a nice fat hen
who will keep us warm.

## PITT POETRY SERIES
Ed Ochester, General Editor

David Huddle, *Paper Boy*
Lawrence Joseph, *Shouting at No One*
Shirley Kaufman, *The Floor Keeps Turning*
Shirley Kaufman, *From One Life to Another*
Shirley Kaufman, *Gold Country*
Ted Kooser, *Sure Signs: New and Selected Poems*
Larry Levis, *Wrecking Crew*
Robert Louthan, *Living in Code*
Tom Lowenstein, tr., *Eskimo Poems from Canada and Greenland*
Archibald MacLeish, *The Great American Fourth of July Parade*
Peter Meinke, *Trying to Surprise God*
Judith Minty, *In the Presence of Mothers*
James Moore, *The New Body*
Carol Muske, *Camouflage*
Leonard Nathan, *Dear Blood*
Leonard Nathan, *Holding Patterns*
Kathleen Norris, *The Middle of the World*
Sharon Olds, *Satan Says*
Greg Pape, *Black Branches*
Greg Pape, *Border Crossings*
Thomas Rabbitt, *Exile*
James Reiss, *Express*
Ed Roberson, *Etai-Eken*
Eugene Ruggles, *The Lifeguard in the Snow*
Dennis Scott, *Uncle Time*
Herbert Scott, *Groceries*
Richard Shelton, *Of All the Dirty Words*
Richard Shelton, *Selected Poems, 1969-1981*
Richard Shelton, *You Can't Have Everything*
Gary Soto, *The Elements of San Joaquin*
Gary Soto, *The Tale of Sunlight*
Gary Soto, *Where Sparrows Work Hard*
David Steingass, *American Handbook*
Tomas Tranströmer, *Windows & Stones: Selected Poems*
Alberta T. Turner, *Lid and Spoon*
Chase Twichell, *Northern Spy*
Constance Urdang, *The Lone Woman and Others*
Constance Urdang, *Only the World*
Ronald Wallace, *Tunes for Bears to Dance To*
Cary Waterman, *The Salamander Migration and Other Poems*
Bruce Weigl, *A Romance*
David P. Young, *The Names of a Hare in English*
Paul Zimmer, *Family Reunion: Selected and New Poems*